QUADRASEX

A UNIPHYSICAL ANALYSIS OF SEXUAL ORIENTATION

YAOUNDE OLU, Ph.D.

ASTROPOINT
Research*Publishing*Consulting
Chicago, Illinois

The author may be contacted at:
astropoint@aol.com
www.astropoint.net

TABLE OF CONTENTS

TABLE OF CONTENTS CONT'D.

INTRODUCTION

There are a lot of misconceptions around the issue of sex. Human sexuality is one of the most potent qualities that human beings possess, which is why poets write about it, commercialization exploits it, and people have their entire lives re-wired depending upon the decisions that they make about it. Individuals relocate because of it, homes are broken up and entire industries are built around sex and sexuality. In this monograph, Uniphysics, the Science of Synthesis, will be used to examine human sexuality.

One of the compelling reasons for writing this book is the revelation in the writings of a teen that I happened to come upon. He is a family member and wrote about the anguish in his soul as a result of a "secret" that he harbored. It became obvious, as he matured, as to what that secret was.

It is easy to dismiss homosexuals and homosexuality with a crass nod and a wink while talking about people making "choices" and thus, deserving what they get. It's another thing altogether, however, to discuss this issue as it impacts youth. This makes it more difficult for the homophobes to explain away. The following excerpt is from an article entitled "Homosexual Teen Suicide" by Kathryn Cooke Payne published December 6, 2007.

"A teenager commits suicide every ninety minutes in the United States (Li Kitts). Suicide is the third highest killer of adolescents (Murphy, Kathryn). There are a multitude of factors that can contribute to the propensity toward suicide. However, some of the groups of young people that have often been overlooked when examining teen suicide are gay, lesbian, bisexual, and transsexual youth, or GLBT. A startling 20-40% of GLBT youths attempt suicide (Li Kitts 264). The answer to why gay youths are at a greater risk for depression and suicide lies in cultural attitudes toward homosexuality. Erik Erikson hopes, "Someday, maybe, there will exist a well-informed, well-considered, and yet fervent public conviction that the most deadly of all possible sins is the mutilation of a child's spirit" (Blumenfeld and Lindop). This hope has not yet been achieved by society, which is steeped in fear. Gay teens are more susceptible to rejection by friends and family, violence, and limitations of helping resources, all of which affect gay teen suicide rates."

I might also add that a disproportionate number of GLBT (gay, lesbian, bisexual, or transgendered) youth are homeless, mostly due to family rejection.

The Kybalion[1] discusses the notion of gender as one of the cornerstones of existence, and indeed, it is. The problem comes in when the notion of Gender is misunderstood. Everything obeys the laws of gender, NOTHING is exempted. Yet, because of narrow definitions and religious bias, clear thinking about this matter is rare. It is my intention to clear up some of the misconceptions regarding this very important matter. I understand, however, that reason does not always prevail with those who are unreasonable, but it is hoped that some warmth, if not light, will be shed, thereby helping to dispel some shadows and myths.

Yaounde Olu, PhD

SEXUAL ORIENTATON VS
SEXUAL PREFERENCE

Let's start from the beginning; of all the qualities that human beings possess, sexual orientation is one in which very few people, if any, have real control. People may decide to respond to their inner inclinations, which brings up the specter of *choice* or *preference,* but preference is not *orientation.* One may *choose* to act on his or her inner urges (orientation), which very often, causes one to live a life of privation. The squelching of self-expression is one of the most egregious acts that human beings subject one another, and its usually because of differing belief systems. People use their belief systems to control others, and very often, they do not really have an understanding of *why* they believe what they believe. They are on automatic pilot, operating on memes, while taking some form of authority as a guidepost. In the case of sexual orientation, blind adherence to religious dogma is usually the culprit, but there is also a natural antipathy between opposites - heterosexuals vs homosexuals, that plays a part in the rampant homophobia on this planet.

THE UBIQUITY OF THE TRINITY

The trinity is the basic archetype of active creation. It is the "motor' that generates new growth, and is symbolized by the triangle (equilateral triangle). It is the fundamental underpinning for the concept known as "six," i.e. sex. Here, the body, mind and soul (3) of one person connects with the body, mind, and soul (3) of a partner, hence six (sex). Sex is the Latin word for six.

The Fibonacci sequence[2] propagates a series of triangles. The third point of the triangle is the vector of intent, and can be predicted if the other sides are known, and this is true when regarding both matter *and* energy. Consciousness follows this construct, and triangulation is the origin of conversation spirals, wherein we start on one topic and end somewhere else completely. The triangle is ubiquitous, and its underlying message, is imbedded in the logos of numerous corporations, schools, and institutions .The language of the triangle is expressed thusly: There are always two points, concepts, or ideas that generate a third point, and this third point represents the positive pole of the beginning of a new triangle, a new foundation, the quad. There is nothing that can manifest in this world as we know it without the dynamic tension that comes from opposites in the process of creating mental, spiritual, emotional, etc., offspring.

THE TRINITY BECOMES THE QUAD

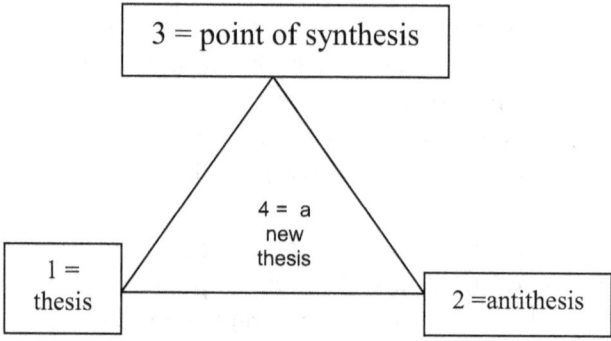

Of course, this idea is not new. The philosopher Hegel[3] offered a version of this idea in the 19th century, but people do not understand that these ideas relate to all *dimensional manifestations*, including everything in our daily lives. The direction of the vector of intent is dependent upon the degrees of origin of two points based on points on a sphere. For example, if point A lies 180^0 from point B, the resultant vector of intent is third point, the synthesis, and it is this concept that is the springboard for new information. Moreover, everything can be placed on a sphere and numerized. *This leads us to understand that anything that we can identify by name can have an opposite concept that is identifiable by name.*

UNIPHYSICS, THE SCIENCE OF SYNTHESIS

Uniphysics is an artscience, i.e., combination of art and science, that takes into account both matter and wave; continuity and discontinuity, and which provides categories for pathways of least resistance traversed by particles, waves, and resulting memes. Pathways, once identified, can be explored as guideposts with which to mitigate patterns of energy, or disturbances in energy fields that are naturally compatible, inimical, or neutral in relation to other patterns, disturbances, or concrete forms of expression.

Richard Feynman, the late theoretical physics wizard, discovered that particles tend to follow the path of least resistance. From a uniphysics standpoint, it is possible to categorize these pathways and predict the probable direction that a particle (person, meme, thought, etc.) *might take in any given situation.*

Uniphysics recognizes "automatic duality" wherein every thought, concept, or idea that exists automatically highlights its opposite polarity. Sir Isaac Newton's Third Law of Motion; every action has an equal and opposite reaction, demonstrates this concept in the physical world. Uniphysics holds that nonphysical concepts also exhibit these reactions, and that nonphysical concepts may demonstrate (e)motion and mass (hypermass). Hypermass is non-physical mass as evidenced in emotions. In other words, thought can be seen to have mass and volume, and these can be identified as memes. Automatic duality is mitigated by finding a third principle, a "point of synthesis" that ties together opposite concepts, whether physical or nonphysical. A point of balance, or midpoint, which serves as a fulcrum, can determine the balance or imbalance of polarities.

Hindsight will find that the new frontier, the missing link that will unify relativity theory and quantum mechanics, will be the mathematics of consciousness. Consciousness is the "tertium quid," the midpoint that unifies the world of matter and that of energy. Thought is energy. Einstein's formula, $E=mc^2$, tells us that matter and energy are actually one and the same. If this is true, as the development of the atomic bomb has demonstrated, it would be beneficial to identify a formula for the interface between the two, i.e., the point at which energy transforms into matter or vice versa. Unimath provides a clue as to the nature of the formula for mitigation.

CONSCIOUSNESS CHANGE AND THE VELOCITY OF HISTORY

The term "velocity" relates to a given rate of speed over a particular distance. The basic formula is $V = ST$, where S is the distance traveled through a given time period, T. Here, again, we see the action of the triangle; i.e., speed and time are the two variables of the triangle that result in a point of synthesis, velocity. From a uniphysics standpoint, the Velocity of History is seen as the angular momentum of the Earth's axial spin counted as days combined with the orbital motion of the Earth around the Sun, counted as years, and this orbital motion varies depending upon whether the Earth is at perihelion (closer to the Sun) or Aphelion. And though Sir Isaac Newton demonstrated mathematically that an orbiting body sweeps equal space in a given framework of time,[4] it may eventually be found that the perception of events differs depending upon whether the Earth is perihelion or aphelion. On a larger note, we can also think about a longer measure wherein the Sun is making its way around Alcyone, the central sun (star) in the Pleiades, and all of this in turn is orbiting the central point in the Milky Way Galaxy. It will probably be discovered that the Milky Way Galaxy is orbiting something even larger, and so on.

Everything from subatomic particles to galaxies and larger structures rotate and revolve, which is why the number pi (3.1415926535...) is so ubiquitous and is found in surprising places. Since everything is orbiting and spinning, composite time, i.e., the combination of spin and orbit, must be components of the velocity of time, and, therefore, history. The velocity of history can be seen as the completion of this action; this is why so-called "progress" or "regress" occur during differing time periods. At certain points there is an acceleration that occurs once a key point is triggered in the hypergeometric space that is a composite of the systems of rotation. (R. Buckminster Fuller has opined that a tetrahedron is the foundation of this hyperpace). It must be kept in mind that time, itself, is an artificial concept based on relative motion, and, therefore, we can determine the velocity of history for our globe. It can be found that larger counts can be determined if we take into account solar, constellational or galaxial rotation, but for our purposes, we will confine our quest to the Earth's axial rotation and its orbital motion around the Sun. As our consciousness expands, we will be able to think about galaxial, universal or multiversal time.

The Velocity of History will give us an indication of the rate of historic innovation and change, and acceptance of new attitudes, for a given time period. When assessing the current attitudes connected with sexual mores, it will be found that there has been an exponential change in the outward manifestation of popular opinion in the last 100 years. Our attitudes, therefore, about sexual orientation are changing at an exponential rate. It will probably only be a matter of time that the quaint notion of discrimination based on it by society's mainstream will take effect. Since all things are relative, however, there will always be the avant garde that will be the leaders and way-showers of tolerance and the laggards bringing up the rear who are reluctant to change. The mainstream are those who are firmly entrenched in the current zeitgeist.

GENDER

A great deal of confusion regarding sexual orientation is related to a misunderstanding of the concept of gender. According to the Kybalion, "Gender is in everything; everything has its Masculine and Feminine Principles; Gender manifests on all planes."[5] This is not the same as the general meaning of the word "sex", which is the physical distinction between males and females. *Sex, in this regard, is only a manifestation of gender on a certain physical plane, wherein gender is found in ALL manifestations of existence.* The word "Gender" is derived from the Latin root meaning "to beget; to procreate; to generate; to create; to produce."[6] Gender, therefore, can be seen anytime anything is produced or produces.

UNIMATH - SUPERSYMMETRY AND THE PROOF OF GENDER IN ALL THINGS

Unimath, utilizing the concept of Increment Analysis, demonstrates a law of digit balance in all things wherein any and every number sequence has increments generating balanced binaries that sum to zero. This is true in all cases. The formula is:

$$\Sigma\Delta n = 0$$

The sum of changes between the increments of all number sequences = 0.

RULES OF INCREMENT ANALYSIS

1. Select a number sequence and evaluate the increments between adjacent numbers so that they become positive or negative in relation to each other. Ignore decimal points and treat the number as a continuous sequence. For example, the reciprocal of seven is a series of repeating numbers 0.01428571...:

$$1 \quad 4 \quad 2 \quad 8 \quad 5 \quad 7 \quad 1...:$$

The increment between 1 and 4 is   +3
"   "   "   4 and 2 is −2
"   "   "   2 and 8 is +6
"   "   "   8 and 5 is −3
"   "   "   5 and 7 is +2
"   "   "   7 and 1 is -6

The resulting number string, therefore, is
+3 -2 +6 -3 +2 -6...

2. Isolate the resulting binary patterns and cancel them to zero, leaving one or more remainders. In the above case, +3 -2 and –3 +2 cancel each

3. other, and the +6 and –6 also cancel each other, resulting in 0.

4. To see the underlying patterns of any sequence or sequence segment that is not a circular number, you add zeros before and after the sequence and proceed with the methodology outlined in number 1 above. The digits will always cancel to zero. (The same is true for any sequence that begins and ends with the same number).

5. Though it is important to keep in mind that each digit is an increment that is ten times more precise than the last in the decimal expansion of numbers, the numbers are taken at face value.

6. For further details on analysis and extracting 2nd, 3rd, or N order sequences from non-circular number segments without adding zeros, see *The Law of Digit Balance.*[7]

Increment Analysis, assessing number relationships between adjacent numbers in numerical sequences, is a technique that I introduced in *The Law of Digit Balance,* wherein it was found that all numerical sequences exhibit incredible symmetries. Increment Analysis is used to identify and synthesize number relationships. It differs from the calculus of sequence differences in that the result of analysis is *__a charged__* *__number line__*. Increment Analysis, a Unimath technique used in Uniphysics, the Science of Synthesis, reveals previously unobserved patterns in ALL number sequences that were heretofore hidden, and where the increments of all whole numbers, or fragments of irrational or transcendental numbers, sum to zero while exhibiting beautiful symmetries. There is a logic and order between adjacent digits in number sequences wherein they increase positively or negatively to each other on face value, even though each digit differs by a magnitude of 10, 100, 1,000 units, etc... This seems to be counterintuitive, even though it has been demonstrated to be true in all cases. The model for the balanced binaries found in increments of all number sequences is:

$$+X \ -X = 0$$

The increments between adjacent *circular numbers*, or revolving number sequences, generate oscillating mirror image number groupings that sum to zero.

Example A:
The increments of the reciprocal of the number **13** (1/13); 0.0766923076923...) =
$$+7-1+3 \ -7+1-3 \ =$$
$$+11 \ -11 = 0$$

Example B:
The reciprocal of the number **17** (1/17)
0.0588235294117647 =
+5 +3 0 -6 +1 +2 -3 +7
-5   -3 0+6 -1 -2+3 -7 =
$$+27 \ -27 = 0$$

Example C:
The increments of **any number sequence**
sum to zero if 0 is placed before and after
the sequence:
C(Euler Mascheroni Constant) =
0.5772156649 0 =
$$+17 \ \ -17$$

Example D:
Coupling constant =
0.085424550 =
$$+11 \ -11$$

Any string of numbers arranged in a circle
will have increments that sum to zero. All
subsequent iterations of the number
sequence will also sum to zero with
balanced binaries.

Example E:
Sequence: **3581264** =

1st Iteration	**+10 - 10 = 0**
2nd Iteration	**+16 - 16 = 0**
3rd Iteration	**+27 - 27 = 0**

Example F:
Sequence: **123456789 =**

1st Iteration	**+9 -9 = 0**
2nd Iteration	**+9 -9 = 0**
3rd Iteration	**+18 -18 = 0**

The concept of the digit balance formula is visually represented by the following:

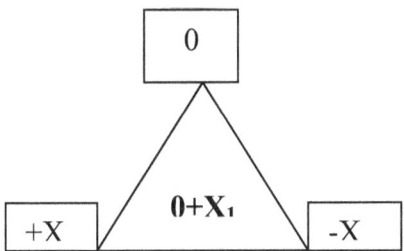

In this diagram +X = thesis; -X = antithesis, 0 = Point of synthesis, and $0+X_1$ = new beginnings, the thesis point (foundation) of a new triad.

21

NUMBERS ARE THINGS

The notion that numbers are things in themselves and have deeper import is not always considered seriously by many people in contemporary society. Sometimes the question even arises as to whether or not numbers were invented or discovered. Mathematician Gregory J. Chaitin of the IBM Thomas J. Watson Research Center, author of *The Limits of Mathematics*, suggests that the structure of arithmetic is random. He states, "Although almost all numbers are random, there is no formal axiomatic system that will allow us to prove this fact." Increment Analysis and the resulting balanced binaries summing to zero tend to refute this logic. Moreover, if numbers can represent things, which they do, if we can believe Plato), then we can conclude that the very model of nature is summed up by balanced polarities that sum to zero, and this includes human relationships. It also connects zero with the notion of fecundity, and not just emptiness.

QUADRASEXUALITY

Nothing can *disobey* the laws of existence and still exist, *therefore, EVERYTHING that exists obeys the laws of existence, or it would not exist.* This goes for the varying manifestations of Gender and expressions of Sexuality. In order for manifestation to occur, the positive must connect with the negative, resulting in a vector of intent (point of synthesis). In this regard, the *concept* represents a fourth point, or foundation.

QuadraSex Model of Human Sexuality

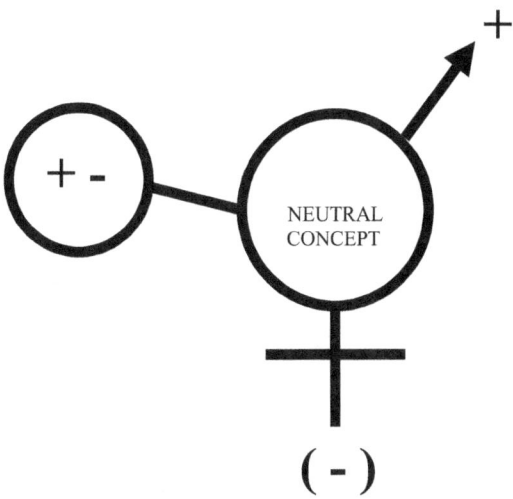

Based on the foregoing diagram of human sexuality, we can identify four basic manifestations of human sexual expression: Heterosexuality (+); Homosexuality (-); Bisexuality (+-), and Neutra-Sexuality (Neutral), or the overall concept of sexuality. It can also represent Asexuality. Gender is represented by the (+) and (-) arms in the diagram. The (+-) and Neutral arms are resultants of the Gender interaction. Shown in another way, we can illustrate the following:

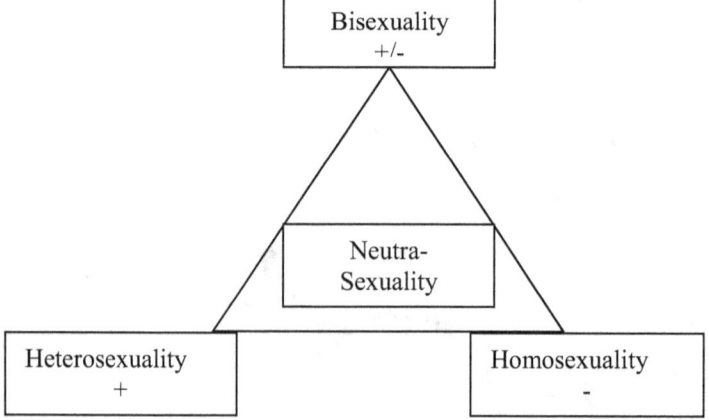

In observing the law of Gender and Automatic Duality, and Unimath, it is impossible to have Heterosexuality without its opposite, Homosexuality, and the resultant Bisexuality. Asexuality is also a part of the human condition. It will probably be found, however, that sexuality operates as a continuum among human beings. There are probably very few pure heterosexuals or homosexuals.

The Sexual Continuum

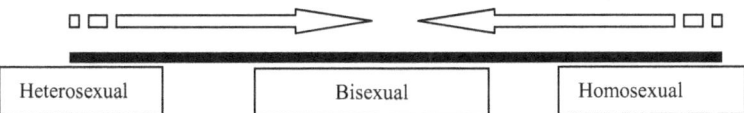

| Heterosexual | Bisexual | Homosexual |

Gender Manifestations

For purposes of this monograph, in the following male/female pairs, I will omit the Point of Synthesis and the fourth point resultants in order to illustrate the concept of Gender in everyday life. Please note that some items are male in one situation, but are female in relation to another. In Gender relations, both sides have elements of each other, as pictured in the Yin Yang symbol.[8] Neither side can claim superiority, after all, what good is a plug without a socket?

MALE	FEMALE
Light bulb	Socket
Plug	Socket
Sun	Moon
Gun	Victim
Shovel	Earth
Metals	Non-Metals
Pens/Pencils	Paper
War	Peace
Up	Down
City	Suburbs
Hot	Cold
Father	Mother
Expansion	Shrinkage
Sadist	Masochist
Screwdriver	Screw
Hammer	Nail
Screw	Wall
Pilot	Airplane
Hammer	Wall
Nail	Hard Surface
Driver	Automobile
Automobile	Road
Foot	Sock
Space Heater	Cold
Foot	Street
Light	Darkness
Body	Chair
Masking Tape	Surface
Person	Room
Space Heater	Room

MALE	FEMALE
Speech	Ear
Wind	Dust Particle
Love	Fear
Love	Hate
Vertical	Horizontal
Bat	Ball
Television	Newspapers
Ball Players	Field
Pool Cue	Ball
Chalk	Chalk Board
Aggression	Passivity
Hot Dog	Bun
Predator	Prey
Earth	Moon
Instructor	Pupil
Lock	Key
Fingers	Keyboard
Flower	Vase
Lamp	Dark Room
Promotional Ads	The Public
Parent	Child
Supervisor	Worker
Principal	Faculty
Vacuum	Floor
Reader	Book
Reader	Newspaper
Dogs	Cats
Hair	Scalp
Home Team	Visitors
Winners	Losers

MALE	FEMALE
Artist	Painting
Individuality	Partnership
Door	Doorway
Eraser	Pencil Mark
Police	Civilians
Pitcher	Catcher
Lightning	Thunder
Action	Reaction
Cathode	Anode
Author	Book
Poet	Poem
Photographer	Camera
Knife	Steak
Push	Fall
Right Side of Male Body	Left Side of Female Body
Sperm	Egg
Phallus	Vagina
Positron	Electron
Proton	Electron
Electricity	Magnetism
Centrifugal Force	Centripetal Force
Glucose	Glucagon
Sympathetic Nervous System	Parasympathetic Nervous System
God	Devil
Good	Evil
Boy	Girl
Positive #s	Negative #s
Androgen	Estrogen

MALE	FEMALE
Left Brain	Right Brain
Right Handedness	Left Handedness
Pimp	Whore
Gas Pump	Gas Tank
Rider	Motorcycle
Odd Numbers	Even Numbers
Light Waves	Sound Waves?
H	0_2
Thoughts	Feelings
CD Burner	CD
Flower	Flower Pot
Breath	Lungs
Consciousness	Brain
Wind	Kite
Voice	Receiver
Water	Cup
Bully	Victim
Groceries	Grocery Bag
Mars	Venus
Software	Computer
Finger	Ring
Arm	Bracelet
Fish	Water
Files	File Cabinet
USB Cable	USB Port
Letter	Envelope
Butch Male	Effeminate Male
Butch Lesbian	Femme Lesbian

NATURE OR NURTURE?

There is a lot of hysterical nonsense surrounding homosexuality which was, until recently, categorized as a mental illness. There are, in fact, a whole cadre of people who feel that homosexuals should not even exist! The truth of the matter is that they exist as a balance in nature's laws. Most homosexuals have heterosexual parents, and sexual orientation is often apparent in very young children. I remember an incident wherein a teacher was repulsed by a 5-year-old male kindergarten student who was extremely effeminate. This child had heterosexual parents, both who were in the home, and there were no gay role models. From whence did his behavior originate? All indicators point to within - to being inborn.

WHY WE BELIEVE WHAT WE BELIEVE: MEMES AND PHEMES

Epistemology deals with the study of the origins and nature of human knowledge. Perception is an underpinning of this concept, because perception tends to lead to reality. However, one of the reasons that people believe what they believe is connected to the notion of MEMES.

Memes are words and concepts that circulate infecting the mind like a virus. Phemes are visual memes. A meme imbeds itself into the consciousness of people and proceeds to replicate itself, over and over, causing behavior modification. For example, many Americans accused the first Black president of the United States of belonging to a Christian church that allegedly spewed hatred against America and against White people. Conversely, many Americans also accused him of being a Muslim. It is not rational for him to be accused of both: he is either a Christian or a Muslim, but not both, yet many bought into this illogical proposition. They were influenced by memes. This is due to the level of emotion surrounding the situation by those who opposed his presidency for whatever reasons. The more emotion attached to a subject in a person's mind, the less rational decision making occurs regarding the subject: This is demonstrated by the following:

$$E \; \alpha \; R^{-1}$$

...where E equals Emotion; α *(the Greek* letter alpha) equals proportionality; *and R equals rationality or Reason. The above statement, therefore, reads "Emotions are directly proportional to the inverse of Reason."*

BELIEVABILITY QUOTIENTS

Believability, on the other hand, is directly proportional to emotion as outlined in the following statement:

$$B \; \alpha \; E$$

The more emotion around a certain subject that we possess, the more we tend to believe that our position is correct.

If $E \; \alpha \; R^{-1}$, and $B \; \alpha \; E$,

then $B \; \alpha \; R^{-1}$,

In other words, belief is inversely proportional to rationality or reason.

Taking this into consideration, Memes influence believability based on the amount of emotion involved.

What is considered Normal during one time period will shift depending upon the duration of the meme. There is, therefore, *a shifting of norms in the context of the velocity of history* that occurs around common memes. This is psychological evolution.

A common meme that has circulated relating to sexuality, and particular, to the renunciation of homosexuality, is "God made Adam and Eve, not Adam and Steve." This statement is not true, since Adam and Steve, as well as Eve and Eva, currently exist in numbers exceeding the hundreds of thousands. That which does not obey the laws of existence can't exist.

THE MAIN STREAM

The mainstream is *the main stream of ideas in a society during a given period in the velocity of history.* It is a region of prevailing "wisdom" outside of which thoughts held become suspect. Lone visionaries who hold ideas outside the mainstream are considered crazy if the velocity of history's momentum has the idea moving in the direction of the mainstream but at a greater speed, thus being ahead of the mainstream's bell curve. Once the idea has been adopted by the mainstream, i.e., once the middle of the bell curve reached the

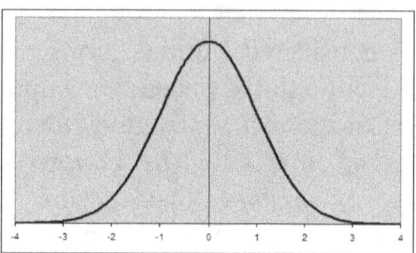

visionaries become classed as prophets. Yesterdays crazies are often tomorrow's prophets.

Mainstream Dynamics

EXTREME CONSERVATIVES (LAGGARDS) (a)	POPULAR IDEAS/DOMINANT MEMES (b)	VISIONARIES AND "CRAZIES" (c)
PAST	PRESENT	FUTURE

(The velocity of history)

THE OPINION BANK

The previous diagram demonstrates the notion that the velocity of time is an important factor in the acceptance of ideas. Pioneers are often ridiculed before the mainstream acceptance of ideas, and venerated after the ideas have been accepted by the mainstream, i.e., at least 51%+ of a population. We can divide this timeline into categories: "a"= archaic thinking (laggards); "b" = current dominant memes; and "c" = avant garde thinking; the visionaries and "crazies," which results in new tradition. Category "a" and "c" ideas are always outside of the mainstream, the "Opinion Bank." An assessment of current mainstream dynamics can be seen in the chart on the next page.

2011 Mainstream Dynamics

BELIEFS IN...	category a	category b	category c
Aliens & UFOs			X
The world is Flat	X		
Astrology*			X
Free Energy			X
Statistics		X	
Viability of computers		X	
In God	X	X	X
Space Flight		X	
Women Voting		X	
Cold Fusion			X
Global Warming			X
Uniphysics , the Science of Synthesis			X
"Naturalness" of Homosexuality			X

NOTE:*The topic of Astrology indicates that the arrow of time in the velocity of history is cyclical, in that there was a time that people believed strongly in astrology. Today it is a category "c" belief).

The velocity of history is fluid, and what is considered mainstream during one time period can be considered backward in another. For example, at one time the mainstream meme was that the world is flat. Today, the mainstream thinking is that the world is NOT flat, that it is an "oblate spheroid." However, even in those earlier times, there were those who believed that the world was not flat. They were the category "c" people during that period. Category "c" people, therefore, are moving at a greater rate of psychological speed than those in the mainstream.

SPECTACULAR EXAMPLES OF MAINSTREAM VISION FAILURES

The following pronouncements were made by reputable individuals regarding thoughts influenced by prevailing wisdom during the time the statements were made. **These *"Bad Predictions about Great Inventions"* were published by "rolacl 2" on the Internet social publishing website Scribd (www.Scribd.com) on March 28, 2006.** These provide outstanding examples of hindsight in poor judgment based on contemporary ideas.

Events

«We will bury you.»
Nikita Khrushchev, Soviet Premier, **predicting Soviet communism will win over U.S. capitalism**, 1958.

- «**Everything that can be invented has been invented**.»
Charles H. Duell, an official at the US patent office, 1899.

- «I see **no good reasons why** the views given in this volume **should shock the religious sensibilities** of anyone.»
Charles Darwin, in the foreword to his book, The Origin of Species, 1869.

- «Stocks have reached what looks like a permanently high plateau.»
Irving Fisher, economics professor at Yale University, 1929.

- «If anything remains more or less **unchanged**, it will be **the role of women**.»
David Riesman, conservative American social scientist, 1967.

- «It will be gone by June.»
Variety, passing **judgement on rock 'n roll in 1955**.

- «**Democracy will be dead by 1950**.»
John Langdon-Davies, A Short History of The Future, 1936.

- «A short-lived satirical pulp.»
TIME, writing off Mad magazine in 1956.

- «And for the tourist who really wants to get away from it all, **safaris in Vietnam**» Newsweek, **predicting popular holidays for the late 1960s**.

- «**Four or five frigates will do the business** without any military force.» –– British prime minister Lord North, **on dealing with the rebellious American colonies**, 1774.

- «In all likelihood world inflation is over.» International Monetary Fund Ceo, 1959.

- «This antitrust thing will blow over.» Bill Gates, founder of Microsoft.

- «**Remote shopping, while entirely feasible, will flop** - because women like to get out of the house, like to handle merchandise, like to be able to change their minds.» TIME, 1966, **in one sentence writing off e-commerce** long before anyone had ever heard of it.

- «They couldn't hit an elephant at this dist-» Last words of Gen. John Sedgwick, spoken as he looked out over the parapet at enemy lines during the Battle of Spotsylvania in 1864.

- «Our country has deliberately undertaken a great social and economic experiment, noble in motive and far reaching in purpose." –– Herbert Hoover, on Prohibition, 1928.

- «It will be years - **not in my time - before a woman will become Prime Minister.**»

Margaret Thatcher, future Prime Minister, October 26th, 1969.

- «Read my lips: **NO NEW TAXES.**»
George Bush, 1988.

- «**You will be home before the leaves have fallen** from the trees.» — Kaiser Wilhelm, **to the German troops**, August 1914.

- «This is the second time in our history that there has come back from Germany to Downing Street peace with honor. **I believe it is peace for our time**.» — Neville Chamberlain, British Prime Minister, September 30th, **1938**.

- «That virus is a pussycat.» — Dr. Peter Duesberg, molecular-biology professor at U.C. Berkeley, on HIV, 1988.

- «**The case is a loser**.» — Johnnie Cochran, **on soon-to-be client O.J.'s chances** of winning, 1994.

- «**Reagan doesn't have that presidential look**.» — United Artists Executive, **rejecting Reagan as lead in 1964 film** The Best Man.

- «Capitalist production begets, with the inexorability of a law of nature, its own negation.»
Karl Marx.

- «Sensible and responsible **women do not want to vote**.»
Grover Cleveland, U.S. President, 1905.

- «Man **will not fly for 50 years.**» **Wilbur Wright**, American aviation pioneer, to brother Orville, **after a disappointing flying experiment**, 1901 (their first successful flight was in 1903).

- «I am **tired of all this sort of thing called science** here... We have spent millions in that sort of thing for the last few years, and it is time it should be stopped.» Simon Cameron, U.S. Senator, on the Smithsonian Institute, **1901.**

- «The Americans are good about making fancy cars and refrigerators, but **that doesn't mean they are any good at making aircraft**. They are bluffing. They are excellent at bluffing.» Hermann **Goering**, Commander-in-Chief of the Luftwaffe, 1942.

- «With over fifteen types of foreign cars already on sale here, the **Japanese auto industry isn't likely to carve out a big share of the market** for itself.» Business Week, August 2, 1968.

- «The multitude of books is a great evil. There is no limit to this fever for writing; every one must be an author; some out of vanity, to acquire celebrity and raise up a name, others for the sake of mere gain.» Martin Luther, German Reformation leader, Table Talk, 1530s(?).

- «Ours has been the first [expedition], and **doubtless to be the last**, to visit this profitless locality.»

Lt. Joseph Ives, after visiting the **Grand Canyon** in 1861.

- «There is no doubt that **the regime of Saddam Hussein possesses weapons of mass destruction**. As this operation continues, those weapons will be identified, found, along with the people who have produced them and who guard them.» General Tommy Franks, March 22nd, **2003**.

Light Bulb

- «... good enough for our transatlantic friends ... but **unworthy of the attention** of practical or scientific men.» British Parliamentary Committee, referring to Edison's light bulb, 1878.

- «Such startling announcements as these **should be deprecated as being unworthy of science** and mischievous to its true progress.» Sir William Siemens, on Edison's light bulb, 1880.

- «Everyone acquainted with the subject will recognize **it as a conspicuous failure**.» Henry Morton, president of the Stevens Institute of Technology, on Edison's light bulb, 1880.

Automobiles

- «The horse is here to stay but the **automobile is only a novelty**, a fad.»
The president of the Michigan Savings Bank advising Henry Ford's lawyer not to invest in the Ford Motor Co., 1903.

- «That the automobile **has practically reached the limit of its development** is suggested by the fact that during the past year no improvements of a radical nature have been introduced.»
Scientific American, Jan. 2 edition, **1909**.

- «The ordinary "horseless carriage" is at present a luxury for the wealthy; and although its price will probably fall in the future, it will **never, of course, come into as common use** as the bicycle.»
Literary Digest, 1899.

Airplanes

- «Flight by **machines heavier than air** is unpractical (sic) and **insignificant**, if not utterly impossible.» - Simon Newcomb; The Wright Brothers flew at Kitty hawk 18 months later. Newcomb was not impressed.

- «Heavier-than-air **flying machines are impossible**.»
Lord Kelvin, British mathematician and physicist, president of the British Royal Society, 1895.

- «It is apparent to me that the possibilities of the aeroplane, which two or three years ago were thought to hold the solution to the [flying machine] problem, have been exhausted, and that we must turn elsewhere.»
Thomas Edison, American inventor, 1895.

- «Airplanes are interesting toys but of **no military value.**»
Marechal Ferdinand Foch, Professor of Strategy, Ecole Superieure de Guerre, 1904.

- «There will **never be a bigger plane** built.»
A Boeing engineer, after the first flight of the 247, a twin engine plane that holds ten people.

Computers

- «Where a calculator on the ENIAC is equipped with 18,000 vacuum tubes and weighs 30 tons, **computers in the future may have only 1,000 vacuum tubes and weigh only 1.5 tons**.»
Popular Mechanics, March 1949.

- «There is **no reason anyone would want a computer** in their home.»
Ken Olson, president, chairman and founder of Digital Equipment Corp. (DEC), maker of big business mainframe computers, arguing against the PC in 1977.

- «I have travelled the length and breadth of this country and talked with the best people, and I can assure you that **data processing is**

a fad that won't last out the year.»
The editor in charge of business books for
Prentice Hall, 1957.

• «But what... is it good for?»
IBM executive Robert Lloyd, speaking in 1968
microprocessor, the heart of today's
computers.

Radio

• «Radio has **no future.**»
Lord Kelvin, Scottish mathematician and
physicist, former president of the Royal
Society, 1897.

• «The wireless music box has **no
imaginable commercial value**. Who would
pay for a **message sent to no one in
particular**?»
Associates of David Sarnoff responding to the
latter's call for investment in the radio in 1921.

• «Lee DeForest has said in many
newspapers and over his signature that it
would be possible to transmit the human voice
across the Atlantic before many years. Based
on these absurd and deliberately misleading
statements, the misguided public ... has been
persuaded to purchase stock in his company
...»
a U.S. District Attorney, prosecuting American
inventor Lee DeForest for selling stock
fraudulently through the mail for his Radio
Telephone Company in 1913.

Space Travel

- «There is practically **no chance communications space satellites** will be used to **provide better** telephone, telegraph, television, or radio service inside the United States.»
T. Craven, FCC Commissioner, in 1961 (the first commercial communications satellite went into service in 1965).

- «Space travel is utter bilge.»
Richard Van Der Riet Woolley, upon assuming the post of Astronomer Royal in 1956.

- «Space travel is bunk.»
Sir Harold Spencer Jones, Astronomer Royal of the UK, 1957 (two weeks later Sputnik orbited the Earth).

- «**To place a man** in a multi-stage rocket and project him into the controlling gravitational field of **the moon** where the passengers can make scientific observations, perhaps land alive, and then return to earth - all that **constitutes a wild dream worthy of Jules Verne**. I am bold enough to say that such a **man-made voyage will never occur** regardless of all future advances.»
Lee DeForest, American radio pioneer and inventor of the vacuum tube, in 1926

Rockets

- «We stand on the threshold of rocket mail.» — U.S. postmaster general Arthur Summerfield, in 1959.

- «... too far-fetched to be considered.» Editor of Scientific American, in a letter to Robert Goddard about Goddard's idea of a rocket-accelerated airplane bomb, 1940 (German V2 missiles came down on London 3 years later).

- «A rocket will **never be able to leave the Earth's** atmosphere.» New York Times, 1936.

Atomic and Nuclear Power

- «The basic questions of design, material and shielding, in **combining a nuclear reactor with a home boiler and cooling unit**, no longer are problems... The system would heat and cool a home, provide unlimited household hot water, and melt the snow from sidewalks and driveways. All that could be done for six years on a single charge of fissionable material **costing about $300.**» — Robert Ferry, executive of the U.S. Institute of Boiler and Radiator Manufacturers, 1955.

- «**Nuclear-powered vacuum cleaners** will probably be a **reality in 10 years.**» — Alex Lewyt, president of vacuum cleaner company Lewyt Corp., in the New York Times in **1955.**

- «That is the **biggest fool thing** we have ever done [research on]... **The bomb will never go off**, and I speak as an expert in explosives.»
Admiral William D. Leahy, U.S. Admiral working in the U.S. Atomic Bomb Project, advising President Truman on atomic weaponry, 1944.

- «Atomic energy might be as good as our present-day explosives, but it is **unlikely to produce anything very much more dangerous**.»
Winston Churchill, British Prime Minister, 1939.
- «The energy produced by the breaking down of the atom is a **very poor kind of thing**. Anyone who expects a source of power from the transformation of these atoms is talking moonshine.»
Ernest Rutherford, shortly after splitting the atom for the first time.

- «There is **not the slightest indication that nuclear energy will ever be obtainable**. It would mean that the atom would have to be shattered at will.»
Albert Einstein, 1932.

- «There is no likelihood man can ever tap the power of the atom.»
Robert Millikan, American physicist and Nobel Prize winner, 1923.

Films

- «Who the hell wants to **hear actors talk**?»
H. M. Warner, co-founder of **Warner Brothers**, 1927.

- «The **cinema is little more than a fad**. It's canned drama. What audiences really want to see is flesh and blood on the stage." — Charlie Chaplin, actor, producer, director, and studio founder, 1916.

Telephone/Telegraph

- «This 'telephone' has too many shortcomings to be seriously considered as a means of communication. The device is inherently of **no value to us.**»
A memo at **Western Union**, 1878 (or 1876).

- «The Americans have need of the telephone, but we do not. **We have plenty of messenger boys.**»
Sir William Preece, Chief Engineer, **British Post Office**, 1878.

- «It's a great invention but **who would want to use it** anyway?»
Rutherford B. Hayes, U.S. President, **after a demonstration of Alexander Bell's telephone, 1876.**

- «A man has been **arrested in New York** for attempting to extort funds from ignorant and **superstitious people by exhibiting a device which he says will convey the human voice any distance** over metallic wires so that it will

be heard by the listener at the other end. **He calls this instrument a telephone**. Well-informed people know that it is impossible to transmit the human voice over wires.»
News item in a **New York newspaper, 1868.**

Television

- «**Television won't last**. It's a flash in the pan.»
Mary Somerville, pioneer of radio educational broadcasts, 1948.

- «Television won't last because **people will soon get tired of staring at a plywood box** every night.»
Darryl Zanuck, movie producer, 20th Century Fox, 1946.

- «While theoretically and technically television may be feasible, **commercially and financially it is an impossibility**, a development of which we need waste little time dreaming.»
Lee DeForest, American radio pioneer and inventor of the vacuum tube, 1926.

Railroads

- «Dear Mr. President: The canal system of this country is **being threatened by a new form of transportation known as 'railroads'** ... As you may well know, Mr. President, 'railroad' carriages are pulled at the **enormous speed of 15 miles per hour by**

50

'engines' which, in addition to endangering life and limb of passengers, roar and snort their way through the countryside, setting fire to crops, scaring the livestock and frightening women and children. **The Almighty certainly never intended that people should travel at such breakneck speed.**»
Martin Van Buren, Governor of New York, 1830(?).

- «What can be more **palpably absurd** than the prospect held out of locomotives travelling twice as fast as stagecoaches?»
The Quarterly Review, March edition, 1825.

- «Rail travel at high speed is not possible, because **passengers, unable to breathe, would die** of asphyxia.»
Dr Dionysys Larder (1793-1859), professor of Natural Philosophy and Astronomy, University College London.

Other Technology

- «Transmission of documents via telephone wires is possible in principle, but the apparatus required is so expensive that it will **never become a practical proposition.**»
Dennis Gabor, British physicist and author of Inventing the Future, 1962.

- «**[By 1985], machines** will be capable of **doing any work Man can do.**»
Herbert A. Simon, of Carnegie Mellon University - considered to be a founder of the field of artificial intelligence - speaking in 1965.

51

- «The world **potential market for copying machines is 5000** at most.»
IBM, to the eventual founders of Xerox, saying the photocopier had no market large enough to justify production, 1959.

- «I must confess that my imagination refuses to see any sort of **submarine doing anything but suffocating** its crew and floundering at sea.»
HG Wells, British novelist, in 1901.

- «**X-rays** will prove to be a **hoax**.»
Lord Kelvin, President of the Royal Society, 1883.

- «Very interesting Whittle, my boy, but **it will never work**.»
Cambridge Aeronautics Professor, when shown Frank Whittle's plan for the **jet engine**.

- «The idea that **cavalry will be replaced by these iron coaches is absurd**. It is little short of treasonous.»
Comment of Aide-de-camp to Field Marshal Haig, at **tank demonstration**, 1916.

- «**Caterpillar landships are idiotic and useless**. Those officers and men are wasting their time and are not pulling their proper weight in the war.»
Fourth Lord of the British Admiralty, 1915.

- «What, sir, would you **make a ship sail against the wind** and currents **by lighting a bonfire under her deck**? I pray you, excuse me, I have not the time to listen to such nonsense.»

Napoleon Bonaparte, when told of Robert Fulton's steamboat, 1800s.

- «The **phonograph has no commercial value** at all.»
Thomas Edison, American inventor, 1880s.

- «If I had thought about it, I wouldn't have done the experiment. The literature was full of examples that said **'you can't do this'**.»
Spencer Silver on the work that led to the unique adhesives for 3-M **"Post-It"** Notepads.

- «Fooling around with alternating current is just a waste of time. Nobody will use it, ever.»
Thomas Edison, American inventor, 1889 (Edison often ridiculed the arguments of competitor George Westinghouse for AC power).

HUMAN BIAS ANALYSIS

The Highest Believability Quotients are those connected with emotional concepts, and the lowest are those connected with purely mental assessment in the mainstream. Religious beliefs are assigned the greatest number of Mentadynes (i.e., units of Mental Energy). Religion includes the category of atheism. In the case of atheism, the religious values assigned are represented by Negative Mentadynes.

Calculating Mentadynes

Mentadynes, units of mental energy, are vibrational signatures of mental concepts. They are articulated in speech, which is created using vocal chords that cause air to vibrate. One of the best indicators of vibrating air connected with speech is the alphabet, the letters used in words. These words have intrinsic vibrational values. What is being measured is the vibrational value of thought connected with ideas. Ancient Science[9] has identified and categorized these sounds and their meanings (see the chapter on Biosonics). The technique of calculating the "Power" of a word is found in "Arrows of Light by John DeQuer.[10] (See the appendix for the technique). I have used the term Mentadynes in this document to denote this mental power. Binaries are determined by assessing increments between the numbers in the "Root".

Category	Root	Mentadynes	Binary
RELIGION	90	10	+9 -9
POLITICS	119	13	+9 -9
LAW	19	2	+9 -9
SEX	41	5	+4 -4

Category	Root	Mentadynes	Binary
EDUCATION	89	9	+9 -9
REASON	77	8	+7 -7
EMOTION	96	10	+9 -9

In the foregoing, the concept connected with the notion of "Sex" has the lowest number of mentadynes, with "Reason" having the second lowest measure. Interestingly,. The greatest number of Mentadynes is demonstrated by Politics, with Emotion, Religion, and Reason, in that order. Law has the fewest Mentadynes. What might be concluded here is that the concept "sex" should be considered in the category of emotion. It is not connected with "reason." The binary (+4 -4) indicates generation, creation, and transformation.

ASSESSMENT OF HUMAN SEXUALITY

Category	Root	Mentadynes	Binary
SEX	41	5	+4 -4
SEXUAL	60	7	+6 -6
HETEROSEXUAL	136	15	+6 -6
HOMOSEXUAL	113	13	+3 -3
BISEXUAL	72	8	+7 -7

When assessing the above human sexuality categories, the only feminine, i.e., even, or balanced Mentadyne category is that related to Bisexuality (8). All of the other are "masculine." When assessing the binaries, however, Homosexuality and Bisexuality are the only "masculine" concepts.

MENTADYNE (POWER) KEYWORDS
Mentadynes identify the "Power" of words.

SEX: 5 = *Key of Religion, Law (Human and Divine), Benevolence.*

SEXUAL: **7**= *Key of Completion, Victory, Comprehension*

HETEROSEXUAL: **15** = *Key of Chronicity; Repeating Cycles*

HOMOSEXUAL: **13** = *Key of Transformation to Another Condition*

BISEXUAL: 8 = Key of *Relative Justice, Stagnation, Idealism, Judgment; equal and opposing forces*

BINARY ASSESSMENT
If we use the keywords attached to the numbers as identified in the section on Biosonics, **the binaries** connected to the sexuality concepts are the following:

SEX: **+4 -4** = *Key of Generation, Realization; Sex Life and Physical Death*

SEXUAL: **+6 -6** =*Temptation, Comfort, Beauty, Affection*

HETEROSEXUAL: +6 -6 =*Temptation, Comfort, Beauty, Affection*

HOMOSEXUAL: +3 -3 =*Union, Synthesis, Marriage, Action*

BISEXUAL: +7 -7 = *Victory, Comprehension, Completion*

ROOT ASSESSMENT

When assessing these same concepts from the standpoint of *Roots (Gross Roots), what nature does to the concept)* by adding the original numbers crosswise, we get the following keywords:

SEX: 41; 4+1 = **5;** *Key of Religion, Law (Human and Divine), Benevolence.*

SEXUAL: 60; 6 + 0 = **6;** *Temptation, Comfort, Beauty, Affection*

HETEROSEXUAL: 136; 1+3+6 = **10;** *Change for Good or Evil, Key of Cycles.*

HOMOSEXUAL: 113; 1+1+3 = **5;** Key of Religion, Law, Benevolence

BISEXUAL: 72; 7+2 =**9;** *Key of Perfection, Wisdom, Prudence, Altruism*

57

RULING FACTOR

When assessing the concepts based on the *Ruling Factors*, i.e., the cause of circumstance, by subtracting the Mentadyne from the Root, we get the following:

SEX: 0: *Ultimate Balance; an emptiness and a fullness that can add new information*

SEXUAL: -1, *Intelligence, Will and Dexterity negatively considered*

HETEROSEXUAL: -5; *Religion, Law (Human and Divine), Benevolence negatively considered*

HOMOSEXUAL: -8; *Justice, Stagnation, Idealism, Judgment negatively considered.*

BISEXUAL: 1; *Intelligence, Will and Dexterity*

OBJECTIVE

When reviewing the concepts based on *objectives*, i.e., adding the Roots to the Mentadynes (Powers), we get the following keywords:

SEX: 10; *Change for Good or Evil, Key of Cycles.*

SEXUAL: 13; *Transformation to Another Condition*

HETEROSEXUAL: 7; *Victory, Comprehension, Completion*

HOMOSEXUAL: 18; Deception, False Friends, Home, Feelings

BISEXUAL: 17; Truth, Faith, Hope

SUMMARY: CREATING KEYWORD STATEMENTS

When using the keywords in sequence from Roots, to Mentadynes, to Ruling Factors and then to Objectives along with balanced binaries, we can get the following sentences related to the INNER MEANINGS of the concepts assessed. In addition, a new concept, that of Volume, is being introduced. The Volume of a word is the number of letters in it, and provides Context.

SEX: 5 +5+0+10 [+4 -4]: *Sex is Law, tempered by Religion, that brings about ultimate balance and Change of Fortune resulting in Generation, Birth, and/or Death. The context, (Volume, 3) is Unity, Synthesis, Action; Marriage.*

SEXUAL: 6+7+-1+13 [+6 -6: *Sexual has as its Root Temptation, Comfort, and*

59

Affection, with a Power of Victory and Completion ruled by a negative Will that can result in a Transformation to another condition through negative temptation. There is a need for control in Temptation, and Affection within the context (Volume, 6) of Beauty.

HETEROSEXUAL: 10+15+-5+7 [+6 -6]: *Heterosexuality is repeated Changes of Fortune related to a negative aspect of the Law and Religion influencing outcomes but with Victory as a reward. Comfort, Beauty, Temptation and Affection are the balancing factors within the context (Volume, 12) Sacrifice.*

HOMOSEXUAL: 5+13+-8+18   [+3 -3]: *Homosexuality is influenced by the use of Religion that can take one to another set of conditions, utilizing judgment that can result in False Friends, Feelings and Deception. The concepts of Balance through Marriage and Synthesis and Action as determining factors within the context (Volume, 10) of a Change for Good or Evil will influence overall outcomes.*

BISEXUAL: 9+8+1+17[+7   -7]: *The concept of Bisexuality is Perfection in the Power of Judgment and Idealism ruled by*

Will and Intelligence along with the objective of Hope and Faith needing balance in Victory and Completion within the context (Volume, 8) of stability.

HOMOSEXUALS AS "CHANGELINGS"

The concept of "Reincarnation" is a category "c" topic when observed from the standpoint of today's mainstream. This idea, therefore, will not be taken seriously by most people influenced by the dominant memes related to this subject. It can, however, provide one of the most compelling reasons for sexual orientation.

There is a book published in 1941 entitled *"The Lord God of Truth Within,"*[11] wherein the notion of "Changelings" is discussed. Consider the following quote from this text:

"Science today divides men and women into three groups, the male, the female, and the intermediate type. The third type comprises people with a woman's instincts ensouled in a man's body, and those with a man's instincts ensouled in a woman's body. Science attributes this intermediate group, or so-called Changelings, to some defect (sic) in gland secretion."

The text goes on to say:

61

These Changelings find themselves in a difficult position in society, for what is right in their world of nature may not be right in the world of man, and when they seek to obey their instinctive nature they may run counter to the moral laws of the Western world." Further, *"Changeling people should not be condemned until they are understood, and medical science is making great strides in this direction."*

Unfortunately, most of the references to "reincarnation" were edited out of the Bible. This is one of the reasons why it is not a mainstream idea today, though that thinking is gaining momentum. Reincarnation, or the notion that we have recurring lives, would go a long way in explaining the inconsistencies in our current lives. This would be especially true for the topic of homosexuality, or Changelings. There are some writers who claim to have forefront knowledge about this say that we sometimes incarnate in male bodies and sometimes in female bodies. Often, a person born in a male body may have a strong identification with an incarnation in which the entity was female, and the memories connected with this favored incarnation carry over into the current incarnation, thus a male might have female feelings. This is one of the best, though admittedly category "c," explanations for the homosexual experience.

The velocity of history, in essence, resides in the psyches of people in a given generation.

THE ROLE OF HOMOSEXUALS IN SOCIETY

It is no secret that homosexuals have contributed a great deal to the cultural upliftment of society. Many great authors, artists, and leaders of our world are rumored to be, or have been homosexual. Some of the greatest names of all time, in Western society, fall into this category.

Quoting further from *The Lord God of Truth Within:*

"But when they live according to their higher instincts, they have a power of introducing beauty into this world of sordidness through music, rhythm, and the arts."

The foregoing is obvious. It has been jokingly stated that if homosexuals did not exist, the arts would disappear. They tend to be obvious keepers and purveyors of artistic consciousness. This might be because they are self-fertilized, i.e., they have a greater balance between the male and female elements within themselves. Homosexuals seem to be disproportionately creative in whatever field they enter. Again, The Lord God of Truth Within:

"In this changeling type the imagination manifests in two worlds at the same time, and their sensitivity is more highly developed than most people would imagine."

FAMOUS HOMOSEXUALS AND BISEXUALS

The following are just a few of the great names connected with the world's homosexual and/or bisexual community:

Alexander the Great
    *Macedonian Ruler, 300 B.C.
Socrates
    *Greek Philosopher, 400 B.C.
Sappho
    *Greek Woman Poet, 600 B.C.
Hadrian
    *Roman Emperor, 1st-2nd c.
Richard the Lionhearted
    *English King, 12th c.
Saladin
    *Sultan of Egypt and Syria
Desiderius Erasmus
    *Dutch Monk, Philosopher
Francis Bacon
    *English statesman, author
Frederick the Great
    *King of Prussia
Lord Byron

*English poet, 18th c.
Walt Whitman
*U.S. poet, author, 19th c.
Oscar Wilde
*Irish author, 19th c.
Marcel Proust
*French author, 20th c.
Colette
*French author, 20th c.
Gertrude Stein
*U.S. poet, author, 20th c.
Alice B. Toklas
*U.S. author, 20th c.
Federico Garcia Lorca
*Spanish author, 20th c.
Cole Porter
*U.S. composer, 20th c.
Virginia Woolf
*English author, 20th c.
Leonard Bernstein
*U.S. composer, 20th c.
Pope Julius III
*1550-1555
T.E. Lawrence
*English soldier, author, 20th c.
Jean Cocteau
*French writer, director, 20th c.
Charles Laughton
*English actor, 20th c.
Marguerite Yourcenar
*Belgian author, 20th c.
Tennessee Williams
*U.S. Playwright, 20th c.
James Baldwin
*U.S. author, 20th c.
Andy Warhol
*U.S. artist, 20th c.
Michelangelo
*Italian artist, 15th c.
Leonardo Da Vinci

65

*Ital. Artist, scientist, 15th c.
Christopher Marlowe
*Eng. Playwright, 16th c.
Herman Melville
*U.S. author, 19th c.
Horatio Alger, Jr.
*U.S. author, 19th c.
Tchaikovsky
*Russian composer, 19th c.
Willa Cather
*U.S. author, 19th c.
Amy Lowell
*U.S. author, 19th & 20th c.
E.M. Forster
*English author, 20th c.
John M. Keynes
*English economist, 20th c.
Ludwig Wittgenstein
*Australian mathematician, 20th c.
Bessie Smith
*U.S. singer, 20th c.
Noel Coward
*English playwright, 20th c.
Christopher Isherwood
*English author, 20th c.
Pier Paolo Pasolini
*Italian film director, 20th c.
Yukio Mishima
*Japanese author, 20th c.
Eleanor Roosevelt
*U.S. stateswoman, 20th c.
Julius Caesar
*Roman Emperor, 100-44 B.C.
Augustus Caesar
*Roman Emperor
Harvey Milk
*U.S. politician, 20th c.
Bayard Rustin
*U.S. Civil Rights activist, 20th c.
James I

*English King, 16th-17th c.
Queen Anne
*English Queen, 18th c.
Marie Antoinette
*French Empress, 18th c.
Melissa Etheridge
*U.S. Rock Star, 20th c.
Pope Benedict IX
*1032-1044
May Sarton
*U.S. author, (1912 - 1995)
Edna Ferber
*U.S. author, 20th c.
Elton John
*English Rock Star, 20th c.
Margaret Fuller
*U.S. writer, educator, 20th c.
Montezuma II
*Aztec ruler, 16th c.
Peter the Great
*Russian Czar, 17th-18th c.
Langston Hughes
*U.S. author, 20th c.
Pope John XII
*955-964
Madame de Stael
*French writer, 17th-18th c.
Martina Navratilova
*U.S. tennis star, 20th c.
Greg Louganis
*U.S. Olympic swimmer, 20th c.
Billie Jean King
*U.S. tennis star, 20th c.
Roberta Achtenburg
*U.S. politician, 20th c.
Barney Frank
*U.S. Congressman, 20th c.
Gerry Studds
*U.S. Congressman, 20th c.
Hans Christian Andersen

*Danish author, 19th c.
Tom Dooley
  *U.S. M.D. missionary, 20th c.
J. Edgar Hoover
  *U.S. director of the FBI., 20th c.
Frida Kahlo
  *Mexican artist, 20th c.
Suleiman the Magnificent
  *Ottoman ruler, 15th c.
Rock Hudson
  *U.S. actor, 20th c.
Sor Juana Ines de la Cruz
  *Mexican author, 16th c.
Ralph Waldo Emerson
  *U.S. author, 19th c.
Candace Gingrich
  *Gay Rights activist, 20th c.
Margarethe Cammermeyer
  *U.S. Army Colonel, 20th c.
Zoe Dunning
  *U.S. Military Reservist, 20th c.
Tom Waddel
  *U.S. M.D., Olympic star, 20th c.
Kate Millet
  *U.S. author, 20th c.
Janis Joplin
  *U.S. singer, 20th c.
Rudolf Nuryev
  *Russian dancer, 20th c.
Waslaw Nijinsky
  *Russian dancer, 20th c.
Ernst Röhm
  *German Nazi leader, 20th c.
Dag Hammerskjold
  *Swedish UN Secretary, 209th c.
Aristotle
  *Greek philosopher, 384-322 B.C.
Paula Gunn Allen
  *Native American author, 20th c.
Angela Davis

*U.S. political activist, 20th c.
June Jordan
*U.S. author, activist, 20th c.
Rainer Maria Rilke
*German poet, 20th c.
James Dean
*U.S. actor, 20th c.
Montgomery Clift
*U.S. actor, 20th c.
Baron VonSteuben
*German General, Valley Forge
Edward II
*English King, 14th c.

Source: http://www.lambda.org

ADDITIONAL INFORMATION

1. The Hebrew Old Testament clearly indicates that King David had a sexual relationship with Jonathan, the son of King Saul.

2. The Hebrew Old Testament clearly documents a sexual relationship between the prophet Daniel and a man named Ashpenaz, and indicates that God put Daniel into that relationship.

3. Much to the embarrassment of the Vatican, the Catholic Boswell has uncovered proof that, up until the fourteenth century, the church was routinely performing wedding ceremonies for same-sex couples.

69

4. The social tides in Europe began to turn against homosexuality around the thirteenth century. Up until that time, there was no organized opposition to homosexuality, either from society or from the church.

5. The religious tide did not turn against homosexuals until after the social tides. The change in society's attitude toward homosexuals was the only reason the church stopped marrying them and began to persecute   them.

6. Boswell found that same-sex marriage continued in certain parts of eastern Europe until the nineteenth century, and that in a few villages, they still continue.

7. King James, who ordered the English translation of the Bible which bears his name, was a homosexual, a fact of which the translators were well aware. This fact displeased them, but since he was the king, they could not express their displeasure openly. Although on the surface, they were careful to be certain that their translation flattered and pleased the king, they also used it to attack him in a way he could not fight.

8. There is absolutely no condemnation of homosexuality in the Hebrew Old Testament.

10. There is absolutely no condemnation of homosexuality in the Greek New Testament.

11. All English translations (one of the earliest being 1611 AD, more than 200 years after the social tide turned against homosexuals, and more than 100 years after the church stopped performing most homosexual weddings) have been deliberately mistranslated to make it appear that God condemned homosexuality.

12. The Hebrew and Greek scriptures never connected Sodom and Gomorrah with homosexuality. The idea that those cities were destroyed for homosexuality is a man-made notion and is unsupported by scriptures.

13. The Greek New Testament, while not condemning homosexuality, does forbid people to attempt to alter their sexual orientation.

14. Both the Greek and Roman Empires considered exclusive heterosexuality and exclusive homosexuality to be abnormal. They believed that all people should be bisexual.

Source: National Gay Pentecostal Alliance Lighthouse Apostolic Church P.O. Box 1391 Schenectady, NY 12301-1391

WHAT DID JESUS CHRIST SAY ABOUT SAME-SEX BEHAVIOR?

Jesus Christ is recorded as having given hundreds of instructions covering behavior and thought; but none of these dealt with same-sex sexual behavior. Jesus concentrated on a person's interactions with God and his fellow humans. He did tell the woman who committed adultery to go and sin no more. But that was the only time he is known to have commented on sexual morality. Jesus may have felt that a homosexual sexual orientation was not a matter worth commenting upon.

Source: Ontario Consultants on Religious Tolerance, Author: B.A. Robinson, www.religioustolerance.org

CONCLUSION

People who are firmly entrenched in their thinking and who are influenced by the dominant mainstream category b, (or category a) religious attitudes towards homosexuality will not, and probably cannot, change their views on this topic, regardless of the amount of reason offered. They will not change their minds until the time comes that either the dominant mainstream religious paradigm shifts, or until they experience sufficient inner growth that will allow them to move away from emotion to reason. Resistance, therefore, is to be expected from them. Category "c" people, on the other hand, might be swayed toward a different viewpoint. And for those Christians who insist that homosexuality is an aberration, it should be remembered that God doesn't break his own laws; if something exists, it must obey the laws of its existence, or it wouldn't exist. It is a well known fact that homosexuality even exists among animals. There are documented cases of this. Consider the following:

"A 1999 review by researcher Bruce Bagemihl shows that homosexual behavior has been observed in close to 1,500 species, ranging from primates to gut worms, and is well documented for 500 of them. Animal sexual behavior takes many different forms, even within the same species. The

motivations for and implications of these behaviors have yet to be fully understood, since most species have yet to be fully studied. According to Bagemihl, 'the animal kingdom [does] it with much greater sexual diversity — including homosexual, bisexual and nonreproductive sex — than the scientific community and society at large have previously been willing to accept.' Current research indicates that various forms of same-sex sexual behavior are found throughout the animal kingdom. A new review made in 2009 of existing research showed that same-sex behavior is a nearly universal phenomenon in the animal kingdom, common across species.[12]"

Those critics, therefore, who insist that homosexuality is not naturally occurring are wrong. Misguided thinking has allowed them a platform on which to exercise unabashed bigotry. In the name of hatred, they condemn those that they do not understand, while accepting outrageous behavior from others in society. For example, some people actually elevate thieves and murderers above homosexuals. This is because there is a great deal of irrational fear and feeling around this subject. As pointed out earlier, the more emotion that exists around an idea, the less logical will an approach to it be.

Another illogical notion is the one that says that homosexual rights are not akin to civil rights for other groups. For example, the Black fight for equality is said to be totally different from the fight for gay rights. This is not true, this assertion is simply a case of emotionality skewing logic. Homosexuality is an *orientation*, and though some people *choose* to go with their feelings, which are inborn, their orientation does not change, just like race is not something that a person can change. Therefore, it is perfectly fitting that the movement for gay rights would stand on equal footing with any other violation of the rights of *inborn* self-expression and/or identification.

Finally, as found in the assessment of the word "homosexual," the vibrational code outlined on page 61 suggests that organized religion is the big influence regarding opposition to homosexuality, and that the issue of gay marriage may play a role in the change of perception of homosexuals.

APPENDIX

A DIAGRAM OF SEX

SEX = SIX
*The triangle pointed upwards is male, and
the triangle pointed downwards is female*

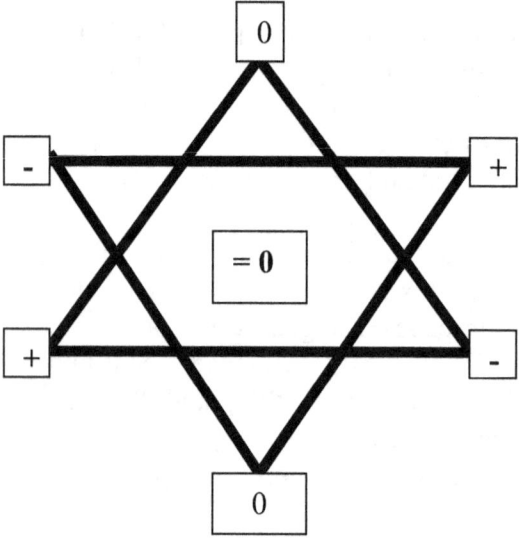

UNIPHYSICS POSTULATES

- Contrary to the Michelson-Morley research, there is a ubiquitous background "ether" that is encoded with information. It is the Sea of Mind.
- The Sea of Mind is a transmitter of intent, and through it we create our reality.
- Every concept or thing automatically makes visible its opposite and bears within itself traits of that opposite (Automatic Duality). This is why independent researchers, authors, artists, etc. often arrive at the same conclusions simultaneously (think Leibniz and Newton; Einstein and Hilbert, Darwin and Watson, etc.)
- Every whole contains within itself an infinite number of smaller wholes and is, in turn, part of an infinite number of greater wholes. In other words, the Universe is fractal based.
- The Universe itself is part of greater and lesser universes.
- Quantar units of differing wholes are expressed by name.
- There is a "People-Flow" wherein every person or thing that we come in contact with brings a message, or provides clues to the category of life

that it represents. This is the holomovement in action.

- Human individuals are the quantar units (minds) of the human element
- Quantar units combine and re-combine according to "valence," or compatibility. On the human level this is seen as "love."
- Quantar units aggregate to form molecules, compounds and mixtures referred to macroquantomly (socially) as families, communities and nations.
- Propaganda is the enzyme that serves as a catalyst for quantar reactions. Propaganda motivates quantar mind by appealing to senses via the element Air, i.e., communications from the environment and internally by impulses generated by genes.
- Propaganda's function is quantar manipulation, which can be mitigated by concepts from differing light (mental) frequencies; mentadynes.
- Thought is focused awareness.
- Thought travels faster than light.
- A neutralizing unification principle (Point of Synthesis) can provide a mechanism for identifying and synthesizing all opposites and contraries.
- Consciousness is focused awareness.

- Ideas are quantar units.
- Ideas are wealth.
- Space, as usually conceived, is non-existent. Its appearance is due to differing scales of perception.
- Every unknown can be understood in terms of a known to which it can be traced by using a law of correspondence related by scalar equivalents.
- Scalar equivalents can be classified; they are co-respondents.
- Life expresses basic evolutionary or devolutionary cycles in spirals and ellipses. DNA, is spiralar.
- DNA is genetic propaganda.
- There is psychological DNA.
- There is no such thing as randomness; there are only causes that are not yet understood.
- Concepts that share similar vibratory rates belong to related sound classes and are expressed in languages as letters.
- Human quantar units (minds) that share similar vibratory rates attract one another through resonance.
- Invisibility can be attained when a quantar mind is on a frequency level that is out of phase with the dominant environmental frequency. This is why many innovators who are deemed "ahead of their time" do

not achieve material success during their time.

- Planned obsolescence, crime and the psychology of limitation are examples of social gravity.
- Movie stars and the Pleiades are co-respondents.
- Quantars generate organic and psychic machines that influence physical laws.
- Quantars attenuate psi currents and memes.
- Each race has its own function in the collective organic entity known as humankind.
- There are relative socio-gravitational "weights" of propaganda quantar units. These can be expressed as believability quotients.
- Naiveté is a propaganda buffer.
- The Force of Propaganda equals Mass(es) influenced by Advertising: $Fp = MA$
- Parents are root gene transmitters and co-respondents.

FORMULAS

$$\Sigma\Delta n = 0$$

The sum of changes in increments of all number sequences equals zero.

$$E \; \alpha \; R\text{^}-1$$

Emotions are directly proportional to the inverse of Reason.

$$B \; \alpha \; E$$

Believability, is directly proportional to Emotion.

$$F_P = MA$$

The (F)orce of (P)ropaganda equals (M)asses influenced by (A)dvertising

$$A_F \; R(X) = PM$$

Advertising Force Repeated X number of times equals Power of Memes.

$$\mathfrak{m} \; \alpha \; T\text{^}$$

The Power of Memes increases in direct proportion to the exponential increase in Time.

$$+\infty \; - \infty = 0;$$
$$0 = 1$$

Positive infinity plus negative infinity = 0; 0 = 1 (The Collective All).

$$\Psi = C^2 \, (\infty)$$

Thought equals speed of light times infinity.

GAGUT

The renowned African Physicist, Gabriel Oyibo, has offered a grand unified theorem that he has termed GAGUT: God Almighty's Grand Unified Theory.[13] In it he asserts that he has been able to solve the problem of the unification of the major forces identified in physics. This is something that has eluded scientists from the beginning of the last century up to the present time, and the great physicist Albert Einstein was seeking a solution to this problem when he made his transition.

The GAGUT equation is:

$$Gij,j=0$$

This is interpreted as GOD (G_{ij}), in GOD's Material (i) and Space Time (j) Dimensions, does not change, where the comma symbolizes change in tensor notation. G_{ij} could also represent everything in the Universe including the Unified Force Field, all of its components, all particles, both atomic as well as subatomic including all quarks, and leptons and all of their interactions.[14]

CONJECTURE: UNIMATH AND GAGUT

As discussed previously, in Unimath all number sequences have increments that sum to zero with positive and negative binaries. *This exactly corresponds to GAGUT in that the sum of all changes in all number sequences is ZERO.*

The question can be raised "Just what do these unimath binaries represent?" When looking at the periodic table and its progression of Hydrogens, there is a sense of similarity between the hydrogen binaries and those in the periodic table. A conclusion might be made, therefore, that the number increment binaries represent *non-physical numerical elements.* In other words, each number string resonates with a chemical element, expressed thusly:

$$\Sigma \acute{M} = H_x,$$

The sum of Mentadynes equals Hydrogens of X number.

One of the basic elements of GAGUT is the reduction of all of the elements in the periodic table to HYDROGENS. It is saying, in essence, that the changes seen from one element to another in the periodic table are merely adding hydrogens. For example, the smallest atom of which we are aware at this time is hydrogen. It has one proton and one electron. The proton has a positive charge and the electron has a negative charge. When we move on to the helium atom we note that it has two protons and two electrons. Additionally, it also has two neutrons, which possess neutral charges. In light of this, we can think of it as being TWO HYDROGENS since the basic hydrogen unit is included twice. The same can be said of the third element, Lithium, which has as its base three protons, three neutrons and three electrons; we can, Therefore, consider that it is Comprised of THREE HYDROGENS. All of the elements can be considered as progressions of the hydrogen atom, so that Gold, for example, can be said to be Hydrogen 79, with +79 protons and -79 electrons, with 79 neutrons. When looked at in this manner, the elements can be seen to be progressions of Hydrogens, as illustrated by the following (the neutrons are not highlighted, but they are present):

+1 -1 Hydrogen - H - **Hydrogen ONE**

+2 -2 Helium He - **Hydrogen TWO**

+3 -3 Lithium Li - **Hydrogen THREE**

+4 -4 Beryllium Be - **Hydrogen FOUR**

+5 -5 Boron B - **Hydrogen FIVE**

+6 -6 Carbon C - **Hydrogen SIX**

7 - 7 Nitrogen N - **Hydrogen SEVEN**

+8 -8 Oxygen O - **Hydrogen EIGHT**

+9 -9 Fluorine F - **Hydrogen NINE**

+10 -10 Neon N - **Hydrogen TEN**

+11 -11 Sodium NA **- Hydrogen ELEVEN**

+12 -12 Magnesium Mg-**Hydrogen TWELVE**

+13 -13 Aluminum Al - **Hydrogen THIRTEEN**

+14 -14 Silicon Si - **Hydrogen FOURTEEN**

+15 -15 Phosphorus P - **Hydrogen FIFTEEN**

+16 -16 Sulfur S - **Hydrogen SIXTEEN**

+17 -17 Chlorine Cl - **Hydrogen SEVENTEEN**

+18 -18 Argon Ar - **Hydrogen EIGHTEEN**

+19 -19 Potassium K - **Hydrogen NINETEEN**

+20 -20 Calcium Ca - **Hydrogen TWENTY**

+21 -21 Scandium Sc - **Hydrogen TWENTY-ONE**

+22 -22 Titanium Ti - **Hydrogen TWENTY-TWO**

etc...etc...etc.., with each positive number representing protons and the negative numbers representing electrons.

Balanced numerical binaries in numerical sequences, then, can be seen to correspond to these configurations and, therefore, are the "thought counterparts" of physical elements. For example, in the repeating number string identified in the reciprocal of the number seven (7), which is +11 -11, we might conclude that this reciprocal is related to Hydrogen ELEVEN, i.e., Sodium. Each number sequence, therefore, can be considered as a "numerical word," which is a manifestation of "light, or thought." These words combine to form sentences, or thought elements, in a similar way that the letters of the alphabet combine to form "sound" sentences. Arrows of Light, a book published in 1930 by John DeQuer, provides a technique for turning numbers into sound. (See Biosonics).

BIOSONICS: THE SOUND OF THOUGHT

Sound is the conveyor of thought. Biosonics is a tool for mitigating propaganda resulting from the force of light (visible thought). Sounds affect matter. The following are values given to 22 human sounds.

SOUNDS, NUMBERS, KEYWORDS, BINARIES

A.... **1**..... Intelligence, will, dexterity/

+1 -1

B..... **2**..... Science, Experience, Analysis/

+2 -2

G..... **3**..... Union, Marriage, Action/ **+3 -3**

D..... **4**..... Realization, Generation, Death/

+4 -4

E..... **5**.... Religion, Law, Benevolence
+5 -5

U - V - W..... **6**..... Temptation, Affection, Beauty/ **+6 -6**

Z..... **7**..... Victory, Philosophy, Higher Mind/ **+7 -7**

H - CH..... **8**..... Relative Justice, Stagnation, / **+8 -8**

TH..... **9**..... Wisdom, Prudence, Altruism/

+9 -9

I - Y - J..... **10**..... Change for good or evil/ **+1 -1**

C - K - CK..... **11**..... Principle of Force, Mystery/ **+1 0 -1**

L..... **12**..... Sacrifice, Expiation, Loss/+1 +1 -2 **(+2 - 2)**

M..... **13**..... Transformation to another level/ +1 +2 -3

(+3 -3)

N..... **14**..... Temperance, Regeneration/ +1 +3 -4 **(+4 -4)**

X..... 15..... Fatality, Chronicity, Coldness/
+1 +4 -5   **(+5 - 5)**

O..... 16..... Accident, Ruin, Energy/ +1 +5

- 6   **(+6 - 6)**

F - P - PH..... 17..... Truth, Faith, Hope/
+1+6 -7   **(+7-7)**

SH - TS - TZ..... 18..... Deception, Home,
Feeling/ +1 +7 - 8   **(+8 -8)**

Q..... 19..... Joy, Happiness, Children, Love/
+1 +8 -9   **(+9 -9)**

R..... 20..... Awakening, Resurrection, /

                                           +2 -2

S..... 21..... Success, Attainment, Power/

+2 -1 -1   **(+2 -2)**

T..... 22..... Failure, Folly, Negation,
Mistake/   **+2 0 -2**

GLOSSARY

Conversation Spirals -- The point in a conversation that spirals away from an original topic due to resultant vectors initiating new starting points of synthesis. This is especially noted when new "memes" are introduced in the conversation.

Fractal diagrams--Mathematical graphs detailing repeating, self-referential structural patterns in nature

Hypermass--Non-physical, but forceful energy, such as emotions.

Implicate Order--The concept, outlined by David Bohm and others, of a deeper level of enfolded reality that describes the universe as a kind of giant, flowing hologram

Memes -- words and concepts that circulate infecting the mind like a virus. A meme imbeds itself into the consciousness of people and proceeds to replicate itself, over and over, causing behavior modification.

Mentadynes -- Units of Mental Energy; vibrational energy given to the sound of words and concepts. This is another name for the "Power" of a word.

Phemes -- Very similar to memes, but are *visual* concepts, rather than words, that circulate infecting the mind like a virus. Fashion fads manifest as phemes.

Point of Balance--Midpoint between two or more astrological concepts that are extremely sensitive to outside influences; a point of dynamic tension, a fulcrum. Force directed toward the Point of Balance can greatly affect change.

Point of Synthesis--Point of blending or cooperation between two or more concepts with a resultant vector of intent. Allows us to see the common bond in opposites or contraries; a unification principle.

Propaganda--A genetic, psychic, or any other type of force or influence that tends to propagate specific behavior.

Quantars (star quantity) -- individual units of mind manifested by all things and concepts that can be named.

Quantarsphere---The Sea of Mind that surrounds and permeates all things in three dimensional space-time.

Scleening - the process of listening and viewing two simultaneous phenomena in order to observe the holomovement. For instance, watching television with the sound turned off while listening to music or another sound source and observing the rhythmic synchrony in the surrounding environment.

Sea of Mind -- the ubiquitous energetic medium in which we exist.

Sex -- six; a *point of synthesis* wherein the body, mind and soul of one person blends with the body, mind, and soul of another, i.e, $3 + 3 = 6$.

Social Gravity - Environmental stressors, i.e., poverty, homelessness, planned obsolescence, unemployment, oppression, and anything that depresses quantar mind.

Teleology--the doctrine that everything is to be understood in terms of its ultimate goal or purpose.

Unimath -- Computational system used in uniphysics. It has been found that all number sequences are balanced by positive and negative binaries summing to zero. This is a demonstration of *SUPERSYMMETRY* in the world of numbers.

Uniphysics, The Science of Synthesis--The blending of physics and metaphysics in a comprehensive artscience.

Words - Numerical wave forms; vibratory propaganda.

CALCULATING POWERS AND ROOTS

The following identifies the method of analysis used in Arrows of Light by John DeQuer [15] to determine the inner meaning of things. This is not numerology; this method focuses on "sound." The chart outlined in Biosonics, the Sound of Thought, in this book, gives the values of alphabetical sounds.

Example: John L. Smith, born February 12, 1892. We begin the analysis:

J O H N L. S M I T H
$10+16+8+14+12+21+13+10+9 = 113$

February 12, 1892
$2 + 3 + 20 = 25$

The Gross Root (G.R.) of the name equals 113. Add these together crosswise and we have a Super Root of 5. Now find the G.R. of the Birth Path (B.P.) by adding all the numbers crosswise. The answer is 25. Now add the G.R. of the name to the G.R. of the Birth Path to get a Theosophic G.R.:
$113 + 25$ equals 138. The Super Root is found by "involving" the G.R. 138; involving means adding the numbers

constituting the G.R. repeatedly until a number less than 22 is obtained. In this case, the Super Root is 12. The Power of a name is found by subtracting the Super Root from the G.R., dividing the product by 9, and adding 1 to the quotient. The "volume" of a name or concept is the number of letters in the name. The "Ruling Factor," the origin of the force, is found by subtracting the Power from the Super Root. The Objective is found by adding the Power and the Super Root.

Any concept can be analyzed using this technique, and it must be remembered that it is the "sound" of the words, names or concepts that we are analyzing. You can add your name to the current date; add a suggested remedy or action for that date to determine a possible outcome, or add any to things together. Once this is done, it is possible to place a set of keywords into a sentence. This is the method used to analyze the concepts of heterosexual, homosexual, and bisexual in this monograph.

ENDNOTES

[1] The Kybalion - Hermetic Philosophy. Three Initiates. Yogi Publication Society. 1912.

[2] Fibonacci Numbers were first demonstrated by Leonardo of Pisa, better known as Fibonacci, in his book titled Liber Abaci published in 1202. In it he discussed the number of rabbits that would be born from a pair of rabbits at the beginning of every month. The resulting number of rabbits revealed the following pattern:1,1,2,3,5,8,13,21,34,55, etc. This series converges to a number called the "golden ratio," which rounded off is 1.618033...This number is found in many places in nature.

[3] G.F.W. Hegel (1770-1831) German idealist philosopher known for his books "The Phenomenology of Mind," "The Science of Logic," and "The Philosophy of Right." His logic had a triadic structure and his system a three-fold aspect. He believed that everything is connected, and is known for the identification of a 3-fold movement of thought termed a "dialectic."

[4] The Kybalion - Hermetic Philosophy. Three Initiates. Yogi Publication Society. 1912.

[5] ibid

[6] ibid

[7] Bowen, Joyce. The Law of Digit Balance. Astropoint Research. 2003.

[8] Yin-Yang represents the ancient Chinese understanding of how things work. The outer circle represents "everything", while the black and white shapes within the circle represent the interaction of

95

two energies, called "yin" (black) and "yang" (white), which cause everything to happen. They are not completely black or white, just as things in life are not completely black or white, and they cannot exist without each other. While "yin" would be dark, passive, downward, cold, contracting, and weak, "yang" would be bright, active, upward, hot, expanding, and strong. The shape of the yin and yang sections of the symbol, actually gives you a sense of the continual movement of these two energies, yin to yang and yang to yin, causing everything to happen: just as things expand and contract, and temperature changes from hot to cold. (http://fly.cc.fer.hr/~shlede/ying/yang.html)

[9] John DeQuer. Arrows of Light. New York.1930.

[10] ibid

[11] The Lord God of Truth Within.

[12] Wikipedia, "Homosexual Behavior in Animals"

[13] Gabriel Oyibo. Grand Unified Theorem. Nova Science. November, 1999.

[14] The essence of the GAGUT Theorem.

[15] John DeQuer. Arrows of Light. New York.1930.